Scrooge's Experiments with Wealth

By Mr. Scrooge

Disclaimer

The author, publisher and all other
individuals involved in the production
of this book are not an investment
advisory service, nor a registered
investment advisor or broker-dealer and
do not purport to tell or suggest which
securities readers should buy or sell
for themselves. They also do no purport
to tell or suggest investment in any
asset class. The author may or may not
have invested in the asset classes
discussed in this book. You understand
that all investments are subject to a
variety of risks. The author, publisher
and all associated individuals assume
no responsibility or liability for your
investment decisions or results.

It should not be assumed that the
methods, tips or techniques presented
in this book will be profitable or that
they will not result in losses. Past
results are not indicative of future
returns, and are not indicative of
future returns which be realized by

CONTENTS

Who Am I?

I am investor by profession (if you can call it a profession). Being an investor means, I don't have to organize my life in the 9 to 5 bracket. Although, I do work tirelessly, but that's just out of habit. I still put long hours at my home office.

When I find a deal I really like, I put in 21 hours a day if I have to until everything gets done. That is just the way I am. I drive a Gallardo, because it was my dream to drive one as a child.

Other than the Gallardo, all my other toys are not really owned by me, but by a company I own. You'll learn why I own most assets via corporations soon enough.

I started playing with money and investments when I was 12 years old. We were really poor, and so I didn't have much. But, I wanted to be rich, because I could not watch my parents struggle and fight over money.

Back then I used to think that money could solve all of our problems. And so I started tinkering with tiny little ideas and businesses. Today, at 27, I am a multi-millionaire and I hope to enter the billionaire club soon.

By the way, I didn't make my money via the internet, like a lot of people claim to have done. Sure, I am beginning to discover the power of the internet.

But, when it comes to business and investing, I have been pretty old school. That's what differentiated me. That's what made me a success.

Before you scream about my techno-phobia, let me tell you, I am a tech lover. Just that I never really thought of using the internet to make money.

But, a few years ago, I was enlightened on the enormous possibilities by a friend and so I have been making a headway in the online world ever since.

My purpose in writing this book is to make as many people aware as possible. Quite frankly, if I could, I would scream at the top of my lungs to everyone who likes to whissss his/her money away listening to bad advice.

It makes me angry, extremely angry, to see people get hurt. Hopefully, this book will make a difference in the lives of people. As I write this, I have already arranged for this book to reach about half a million readers who read books on business and investing.

It won't put a lot of money in my pocket, but hopefully it will put money in their pockets, and wealth will grow in their lives.

What to Expect From This Book

There are a lot of ways to become wealthy. And I will explore a lot of different ways. I am sure, you will like one of the ways and soon be on your path to prosperity.

Over the years, I have experimented with a lot of things, in order to reach my financial goals. I have experimented with gold, silver, stocks, bonds, real estate, private equity, buying small businesses, etc. etc.

Over time, I have met a few mentors too. And so, I wish to consolidate all of the know-how that I have, and compress it into one book.

This book is going to be compressed yet comprehensive, i.e. comprehensively compressed. That's a nice oxymoron, "Comprehensively Compressed".

It will not just provide a general idea, like a lot of books have done in the past. Instead, it will go into specifics, so that you can be made aware of what needs to be done.

And what problems to look out for. In short, it will give you a pathway, and the supplies you would need to stay safe while travelling down that pathway.

The best part about this book is that you don't need to read it from cover to cover. You can simply refer to the chapter that concerns you.

For example, let us say, your slick broker tries to stick a bunch of junk bonds down your throat. Bonds that pay 15%. You get all excited, because your bank is giving you less than 2%.

And the stock market isn't a sure thing. But, bonds are. (Or are they?) So before you dump your hard earned money into an investment, you might just want to refer back to this book.

There is a nice little chapter on the basics of investing at the very beginning, and there is a chapter that goes into the specifics when it comes to bonds.

What's more? The language is easy to understand, so that you don't get lost in jargon. So, this is more of a reference guide than a book you read in one sitting.

Finally, please understand that this book will not make you rich in a day. But, it will make you wealthy. If you can find a scalable formula for success, you can even earn millions. All the Best!

Basics Of Investing

This is by far the most important chapter in this book. If you do not do anything else that is mentioned in this book. At least read this chapter once a year.

Hopefully, just to get your head straight. Also, anytime, some slick wall streeter tries to sell you the next big idea, come back to this chapter, and read it. This will help you keep your focus in the midst of an exciting offer.

I don't make my investment decisions based on external stimuli, and neither should you. Your stock broker, the hot business news anchor, the "friends" on discussion forums, everybody is out to manipulate you.

Let us get one thing straight, real news in America can only be found on sarcastic comedy shows. The real news, gets lost in the midst of over-analysis, propaganda and greed.

So you should be skeptical about any investment advice or even a hint that comes from any external source.

So, does that mean you need to shut your eyes and ears to information? Of course not. In fact, you should know everything about the business world. The fact is, thanks to the internet, you can always get to the bottom of things.

If one business news channel tries to sell you on an idea, you can always change the channel, or go online and check if a news is true.

Even if the news were true, why shouldn't you invest because of the news? The short answer is, because hasty decisions is not something an investor does.

Anybody who tries to rush you, probably wants to sell you something that's not worth the money they are asking for it. So never rush. By staying on top of the news and verifying facts, you will always stay one step ahead of the herd.

So stay aware, but stay cautious.

Use google finance and Reuters for business news. They provide raw news. Refer to SEC filings, in case some odd news comes out about a company.

Have a property checked out by a professional for everything from bugs to cracks in the foundation. Have the person checked out if you are about to go into business with someone.

It all seems like a lot of work, but it isn't. And it's not expensive either. Before investing time, money and resources, that are worth hundreds of thousands, or millions, or whatever the amount is, you better spend a few bucks getting everything checked out.

Because once the transaction is done, you may not see your money ever. What's worse, If you buy a bad house, a bad business or a bad stock, you stand to lose everything.

Now, that you know that you should not make investment decisions based on external stimuli, let us ask another important question? How do you decide to invest in something?

The answer is... Mathematics. Logic plays no part when it comes to a lot of investment opportunities. For example, why would a world class athlete pawn his super bowl ring for "chunk change"? Makes no sense to me.

But, the fact is some players do lose their rings to pawn shops. And when they do, the pawn shops benefit. What is more? A guy like me walks in, and haggles the pawn shopper till he sells the ring for a little more than "chunk change".

Of course, mathematics does not always make sense to people. Instinct matters too. But, if you really want to be wealthy, you should care about the numbers first. If the numbers seem good, yet the person selling you the deal seems shady, walk away!

So, rely on mathematics, not sentiments to make investment decisions.

For example, the next time you hear a rumor about some stock. Maybe you just check out the company on the web first. Even then, if for some reason, you can't restrain yourself (trust me, it will take some time to find your "Zen"), make sure you put in only what you can afford to lose.

Don't bet the ranch on an investment.

To me the number that I can afford to lose hadn't always been zero. But, after a couple of initial bumps in which I saw the middle man earn a nice fees, whereas I lost my money, I realized that I needed to pay minimal or no fees. And that I needed to NOT lose any money. So the number that I could afford to lose became zero.

Today, I can't really afford to lose money. I am set for life. Does that mean that I or you shouldn't take risks? Of course not. I took risks, and really big ones at that.

But, the fact is, I had a buyer lined up, before I bought something. The risk for me was that the buyer might walk away from the deal. As long as I can exit profitably, I am willing to take on a risk. Similarly, you should take risks too.

The fact is, you will never really succeed in business, if you don't risk everything for your dream. But, investing is different. In investing, if you do risk everything, you will probably lose everything. Your motto should be "Live Today, Fight Tomorrow". So the lesson is that don't bet the ranch on anything.

The next tip is that you should learn to develop patience. We have become so impatient that even a few seconds of delay seems like an era to us.

Anybody and everybody thinks of himself as an investor. To most people, long term investing means a year (in theory), and a few days (in reality- because that's how long they like to hold on to a stock). The term "Long term investing" is wrong. Investing by its very definition is long term.

There is no such thing as short term investing. Here is a small chart which shows what long term means to different people:

S.No.	Type of person (based on financial situation)	Meaning of Long-Term when it comes to investing
1.	The average Joe (A target for brokers, TV shows, etc.)	1 Year
2.	The self-proclaimed sophisticated investor (earns a lot of money, and whisses it away) (The main target for all the analysis on TV and online)	5 Days
3.	Wealthy (Self Made)	10+ Years for Stocks, 20+ years for other assets.
4.	Super wealthy (The infamous 1%)	100+ Years

The above table is a reality check for people who proclaim to be sophisticated investors. They like to talk as if they were a billionaire, because they earn an annual income in the six figures.

They are the targets of all the ad campaigns that promise high returns. They are the people who make the broker rich, the banker rich, the mutual fund manager rich, the professional trader rich, the... well you get the idea.

And the worst thing is, because they get paid regularly, they don't think of a loss as a "loss". What the self-proclaimed sophisticated investor does not realize is that had he just put his money into a simple savings account, he would have been able to leave his job sooner and live a "free" life.

What can I say, I get really angry, because I know some really smart people, who went to the best schools, and are still paying their student loans even after earning well.

I really wanted to go to a nice ivy league too, but I had neither resources, nor the inclination to take on insurmountable debt. But, it hurts to see these people keep themselves poor even though they earn enough to actually be completely financially free.

If I remember correctly, Mr. Lynch had also mentioned these people in his famous book, "One Up On Wall Street".

The above table also shows that the average Joe is also the target for various campaigns. But, fortunately he can't afford to act like a sophisticated investor (Thanks Heavens) because of his low earning potential. Thankfully, financial firms have also put in checks and balances to ensure that the average Joe doesn't get burned.

But, the wolves got to average Joe in the period between 2003 and 2008. He was promised the American dream, and handed out a nightmare instead.

But, let us not lose our focus. This book is not about social problems. It is about wealth.

The above table also shows that the wealthy people- people like me who are millionaires (mostly self-made millionaires), tend to have an investment horizon of about 10+ to 20+ years, depending on the kind of investment.

This is because, self-made millionaires want to see their wealth grow exponentially within their lifetime. Let me also say, that unless you can touch lives of a lot of people, you won't be able to make a penny.

But, the most important thing that the above table shows is that the top one percent of the wealthy people in America have a horizon of well over a 100 years. Why? Because they want to stay wealthy. Many of these people no longer directly impact people's lives, and have drawn the scourge of the common man in the past decade. But, you need to step back and think about how they are multiplying their wealth. There is something to learn there.

The super-wealthy impact all of us. Some of them are part of the elusive Federal Reserve, which is central to our economy. Some of them invest in private companies via private equity, helping these companies grow and become global brands.

Some of them help launch startups, fueling entrepreneurship and hence job creation. What "the socialists" don't realize is that the super-wealthy make the economy what it is.

When they buy government bonds for a hundred years, those governments are then able to use that money to protect the country and run it well.

Having taken a detour from our main point, let me return to it now. The point is that you need to have an investment horizon of at least 10+ years when it comes to stocks, and a horizon of at least 20+ years, when it comes to various other asset classes.

Sure, flipping assets is great too, but generally you need to take care that you stay invested in an asset for the long term, i.e. 10+ years. Staying investing takes a lot of patience and so you need to develop patience.

One way to develop patience is that you need to maintain "illiquidity" and get used to the idea that a certain amount of your wealth must never be touched.

If you can't get the money out, you can't whisss it away now can you? Another way to develop wealth is by slowing down your research process.

No investment opportunity is so important so as to demand immediate action. This does not mean that if such an opportunity comes up, you should not take advantage of it. But, action should follow due diligence and not the other way around.

I am human too. And I get excited just like you. There were times when I would see a great house up for sale for a really low number. But, I never left my process and neither should you.

Due diligence first, investing later. I look for reasons NOT to invest, instead of looking for reasons to invest. This is extremely important to remember.

Look for reasons NOT to invest, instead of looking for reasons to invest.

Finally, just because you keep your investments untouched and illiquid, does not mean that you can't have fun. Just like you can get a line of credit for your business or on your home.

You can get lines of credit for stocks and bonds and other things too. So, in case of an emergency or a really genuine deal you can actually get the money you want when you want it using a line of credit.

I actually cannot believe how many people burn their wealth by taking a line of credit out on their houses and then wasting the money on useless toys. Use the line of credit as your best friend and not your worst enemy.

So, take out a line of credit if you feel like you would need the money. But, make sure you use it wisely and pay back the money you use from it promptly.

A credit card is an unsecured line of credit too. But we all know how dangerous it can be. The same goes for any kind of line of credit. So, a line of credit is a way to have money while your investments are working for you. Use it wisely.

Here is list of things to keep in mind:

1. Greed is not good. Don't be a gecko.
2. Buy and forget is the best strategy for any investor.
3. Develop the ability for independent analysis. Not even a penny should be invested before proper due diligence.
4. Stay illiquid, i.e. never touch your investment corpus.
5. Be patient.
6. Don't jump from one stock to the next. Stay invested or don't invest at all until you develop the discipline to stay invested.
7. Stay out of personal debt. Get out of personal debt.
8. Reinvest any earnings/dividends until you have enough. And even then continue reinvesting.
9. NEVER refinance a loan, unless you want to stay in debt forever. Instead find a way to pay off the loan as is and fast.
10. Become a net lender, instead of a net borrower. Government bonds, corporate bonds, etc. are good places to start.
11. Become an angel. Well sort of. Anyone can put up some money via crowd funding platforms such that you get a hefty return. Equity is still the best place to get wealthy.

Enabling inventors and small businesses via crowd funding and other similar platforms, helps make the country stronger. Plus, you can agree to terms that provide better and guaranteed returns. Something that stocks don't promise and the bonds can't really pay.

12. Invest in personal equity. If you decide to become an investor in a startup or a successfully running small business, make sure you invest in the person running the business. But, also make sure that once you become a part of the business, systems are put in place so that if tomorrow this person leaves, you can still have someone else run the business.

13. Remove the psychological barriers. You only know what your limiting beliefs really are. The truth is there is infinite money floating around these days. There is an infinite number of opportunities waiting out there.

14. Break the unwritten rules. But, never break any laws. There is always a legal, ethical way to get the results. So follow that path instead of following the bad advice.

15. Surround yourself with successful people. People with limiting beliefs indirectly impose those beliefs on you. But, people who are successful don't have those beliefs.
16. Be on your guard at all times. Look- family, friends, society, other investors next door, all these people can be assets or they can be liabilities. You don't have to dump them, but you can ensure that their beliefs don't become your beliefs.
17. Find mentors. I know a lot of authors recommend finding A mentor. I don't think you can afford to have just one mentor. That's not how life works. Unless you are like Bill Gates, who had become Warren Buffett's apprentice early in Gates' life, you would need to find different mentors at different stages of your life.
18. Give back to society. This is the most important thing. Even though society tried to muzzle your dreams when they were in their infancy, even though some of your friends may not have believed you, even though some people may have deliberately tried to slow down your growth, the fact is that nothing says you've made it, like giving back to society. My family made my life hell when I wasn't

making any money, until one day an emergency required a big wad of cash. And guess who had that cash? I recently went back to my old neighborhood. I am building a proper school there. Guess what all those people who told me that I was stupid to dream say now? You have to give back anonymously too. But, my point is, everyone would like to tell you what you can't do, until you do it. After that, they'll wait for you to fail and fall, but if you never do, they will accept your way of life.

19. Stop trying to fit in. It is hard to get out of the normal mindset that people have. Do not ever try to fit in. You don't have to do a job just because people around you go to a 9 to 5 job. You don't have to invest in that apartment where your neighbor is investing. You certainly never have to buy the stock that everyone else is buying. The fact is, it makes sense to do things differently, because you avoid average results by avoiding average pathways to success.

20. As soon as you can, get a lawyer to be part of your team. You can't know everything there is to know, and you may make a mistake that could cost you dearly. As you grow wealthier

you can get bigger firms to represent you. And sue someone if you have to. Don't be afraid of the legal process. Unfortunately, the legal system requires that people have deep pockets. But, people should learn never to mess with you. If you don't get legal representation, sooner or later someone is going to force you to get one, and you may not be able to find the right firm or professional to suit your requirements. Don't wait for someone to sue you.

21. Get an accountant ASAP. It is one thing not to have a lawyer on your team, it is totally another if you don't have an accountant. I don't know why, but the self-proclaimed sophisticated investors always have an accountant and somehow they still manage to screw up their finances. The fact is you need a guy you can build a long term relation with. Accountants are good people, treat them like people and not geeks. In fact a good accountant can actually make you wealthier faster. And they know the relevant laws too, so he will protect you. But only if you keep in touch with him. Don't just show up when you want to file taxes.

If you stick to my advice, you will be a millionaire sooner than the experts would have you believe. Nobody wants to tell you that you could be financially independent in less than 5 years if you do the right things.

If you realized that you could pay off all your debts within just 3 years, the banks would be out of a job. Brokers will be out of a job. Refinancing would go out of fashion. But of course, "they" make sure you don't get out of debt.

To me financial abundance is more important than buying a toy.

Imagine, 3 years from now you become completely debt free. You then become a net lender. And a net positive investor. In a matter of a few years, you fire your boss and never really have to work again.

Of course, that's a misnomer. You always have to go back to work. How long can you really stay on vacation? Plus, financial independence does not mean financial abundance.

Financial abundance means having enough so that not only can you meet your expenses. Rather, you could, if you want, increase your expenses as much as you need to and not run out of resources.

Financial abundance is extremely important. It is the actual dream that you should have. Not just independence, but absolute abundance. And the basics of investing mentioned in this chapter will help you achieve financial abundance.

My Experiments With Gold

Gold is that nice shiny yellow metal that does not rust or rot or degrade over time. This means that if someone were to dig up a grave of a Viking ruler or an Egyptian pharaoh, they'd find that everything has corroded or eroded, except gold!

Gold is one of the few assets in the world which has held its value over the past 5 millennia, and it will continue to hold its value.

But why is Gold valuable? Well it all comes down to supply and demand. There is very little gold in the world, but the demand for gold is ever increasing.

Gold can be given any shape or form as desired and takes up so little space that it seems more practical than to store cash for any lengths of time.

The value of gold is also increasing because fiat currencies including the dollar are failing us. The recent decline in the Russian currency is due to the internal problems caused in that country post sanctions, but the fact is that ANY currency in the world can and eventually does move towards a value of zero. That's the truth. The Chinese know this truth. That is why the Chinese government as well its citizens are accumulating gold on a massive scale.

In fact you could actually buy gold really cheap from a lot of banks in Hong Kong, something that is unheard of in the west. The Indians are accumulating gold too.

But, the demand there is more from the people than from the government. Their government is trying to curb import of gold, but Indians are ready to pay heavy duties in order to import gold.

This tells you the power of gold. People are willing to pay any price for the yellow metal. And it's not just these countries. Across the world, people are accumulating gold, because that's where the real value is.

The "powers that be" have been trying to move people off to fiat currencies, and so countries actually get punished when gold imports increase.

They want you to believe in the value of a piece of paper, because they can print as many papers as they want. Plus, a lot of countries are making the economists really angry by completely ignoring the dollar in their transactions.

Countries are trading using gold. We don't like Iran that much, but sanctions had little effect in that country. Instead of trading using dollars, they started using gold and other similar valuables.

And who is buying the oil from Iran even after Uncle Sam told everyone to ignore them? China and India- The two countries who are building up their gold reserves.

As an investor, I don't favor gold over currencies or vice-versa. All I really care about is will I get a great return on investment or not.

The fact is gold fluctuates in the short term, but in the long term, the value of gold increases enormously. What's more? The spot price of gold is the same across the world, which means I can buy gold in Hong Kong and sell it to some pawn shop in Ohio.

Of course, sellers charge a bit extra over and above the spot price. But, that premium is the minimum in Hong Kong and in Dubai. So, gold is cheaper there, as compared to other places in the world.

Spot price is the price of gold at that very moment, decided by the market. So when you see gold at $1100 on a ticker, that's the spot price for an ounce of gold.

And here is another interesting fact about gold. It always keeps up with inflation. That means it always maintains its value, unlike the cash you have got stuffed in the mattress.

10 years later that cash will be worth less, whereas gold will still be worth its weight in gold. And with the tips mentioned by me in this chapter, you would not only be able to profit from gold, but you'd be able to get seriously rich.

Gold is also something that can help you to maintain your investment capital. It is illiquid enough so that you can't spend it immediately, yet it's not so illiquid that you can't sell it in an emergency.

Plus gold prices fluctuate much more slowly as compared to share prices. So, although I would never want anyone to trade in stocks (they should invest not trade), I am fine with people trading gold.

How and Where to Buy Gold

I would not recommend buying gold from any banks in any countries, except for the banks in Hong Kong. All other banks charge so much premium, that you'd have to wait for a hundred years to get your money back.

I would also not recommend investing in funds, considering that you can't actually go and check if the gold fund really has gold in its vaults.

I trust the physical form of gold, bought from either Jewelry shops or pawn shops, whichever is cheaper. Gold comes in 10 carat, 14 carat, 18 carat, 22 carat and 24 carats.

For investment purposes you should generally buy physical gold in the form of bars or coins that is at least 22 carats. Either the bars or coins that you buy should come with a certificate.

Or if you buy it off of some shady character (which I hope you don't) you should know where you can get the gold graded for purity.

You can visit www.ngccoin.com if you want to get your gold graded, tested and certified.

Other than that, if you want quick acid tests for gold, many such tests are available on amazon and in retail stores across the country. Here is a list of products on amazon, click here

All you need to do is rub the coin on the surface and pour a few drops of this acid. And voila! Real gold would not corrode, whereas fake gold would just get eaten up by the acid. The products don't cost more than $10 and are the cheapest way to test gold.

No seller would ever sell you gold at spot price. But, you still need to find someone who would sell you gold cheaper than others. Find such a seller and buy gold from them when gold prices fall.

As we speak, gold prices are fairly low. So accumulation of gold is a top priority for anyone who wishes to invest in gold. And the prices will stay fairly low for a few months.

So, you don't have to rush to buy your gold. But, accumulate as much gold as you can every time gold prices go down by 15%. That is the time you should buy. Gold has a tendency to move in a certain range.

Over the years, this whole range is moving upwards generally, which means the average price of gold is increasing every year. But, what you are trying to do is buy gold cheaply when it's down.

Gold goes through the highs and lows at least twice a year. And unlike stocks, gold rebounds only after a few months. If gold goes down by 15% and you buy.

The moment gold would come back to the same level, you would instantly have made nearly 18% profits. Do this twice a year, and you have a nice 36% profit (pre-tax). Now that's the trading profit. What if you just held on to gold?

Remember I told you that real investors hold on for at least 10 years. If you had bought gold in 2004 and sold it today, you would have made 3X profit.

But, wait. If you had been lucky enough to sell at the top of the market, you would have made a 5X profit!

There are charts that go back a hundred years as well. And what you'd realize is that gold would have given you a 3-5X profit if managed well. Of course, what matters is that you should be able to buy gold when it falls.

Let me also clarify that gold markets are manipulated by certain people as well. So, you need to guard yourself against any news item or experts who tell you to "Buy" gold at certain times, and "Sell" at certain times. Gold is a hedge against inflation.

If you hold 10 ounces of gold today. Buy and sell gold as much as you like, but make sure that at the end of 10 years, you still hold the 10 ounces. This is important.

Because one piece of gold is the same as another.

The amount of dollars that are put up against the gold does not matter. Gold matters. The amount of gold you hold matters. The value is in the weight and purity of gold, not in the dollar value it represents. So just like capital needs to be conserved, so does the amount of gold you hold in your portfolio, in terms of weight.

Personally, I never sell gold once I buy it. Technically, my balance sheet will show that the amount of gold I own has remained constant in terms of weight since 2011.

But, what that balance sheet does not tell you is that between 2012 and now, I have made nearly a 100% over and above the money I had invested gold. You can do what I do.

Or, you can simply buy and forget about it for years to come. I don't think that you should trade in gold often if you don't have the relevant experience. Buy and hold (a.k.a. forget) is the best strategy here too.

My Experiments With Stocks And MFs

I am sure a lot of people will open this chapter first. Stocks have been in fashion ever since the stock exchanges came into existence.

After the internet made it possible for people to trade stocks from the comfort of their homes, that is exactly what people started doing. Of course, the only real beneficiaries of these online trades have been the brokerage firms themselves.

The picture is a bit different when it comes to mutual funds. Mutual funds are generally regarded as safe investments. They are well diversified and cheap, as compared to buying individual stocks to match the fund's portfolio. But are they really worth the fees that the fund manager's charge?

Fees? What Fees?

The most annoying experience for an individual investor is that of purchasing a stock or a mutual fund and getting robbed off of the hard earned money in the form of brokerages and other fees.

So, basically, brokerages put a dent in an individual's portfolio at the very beginning. The lesser money you have, the more punishment you receive.

I remember the time when I had barely earned enough money to trade. This is the time period of my life when I was about to realize how trading was a loser's game. My trades were small because I had little money and for the first few months, I couldn't really make as much profit as I would have liked. I couldn't understand why. Then, I rummaged through all the trades looking for a reason, and then it dawned on me, "THE FEES!"

I opened up the brokerage structure offered by my broker and realized that because I had been buying low quantities of stock at low prices, I was killing my own profits! If I remember correctly, the brokerage along with the other tidbits that they charged, cost me about 2% of the invested amount, ON EVERY PURCHASE! And what's more, in order to entice traders to sell on the same day, the brokerage firm had made the closing transactions free. This meant that if I bought and sold the same stock on the same day, I would actually pay just 1% instead of the likely 4% (2% while buying+2% while selling).

But, was it an incentive or a trap. I realized that it was an unfair trap, due to which a lot of people must have lost a lot of money to brokerages. How you may ask? Because, if you sell a stock on Friday, and it's still a good stock, you are going to buy the same stock again on Monday, and then sell it off by the end of the day.

This increase in frequency of trades would kill your account, because you really just have to do this for a little over a month and lose all of your money. Loss=100%. Of course, the brokerage firm won't tell you that little secret.

That is why, when it comes to trading, leave it to the pros. If you have little money, go for mutual funds instead. Invest a little every month till you grow old... Right?

But, wait. I almost forgot. Mutual funds charge you fees too. Some mutual funds charge a certain amount as soon as you buy the fund. This is known as an "Entry Load".

While other mutual funds charge a certain amount as soon as you sell the fund. This is known as an "Exit Load". The best kind of funds are the ones that have a good exit load.

So that you don't pull your money out soon. On top of that, each year they charge you a fees just for the privilege to do business with them. Vanguard has some of the best index funds on the market, and they have no entry loads and no crazy annual fees to cut your profits.

Look at this example below which provides just another way to understand how MF fees can greatly diminish your returns over the years:

Let us say that Bob starts investing in a mutual fund at the age of 23. Bob is smart, and he buys a mutual funds that seem to have given a return of (say) 13% a year.

Notice, I didn't say invest in a mutual fund, because most people jump from one MF to another, as fast as you can sing jingle bells. And that is not investing.

So, Bob honestly and dutifully puts in a hundred dollars each month for the next 13 months. Out of curiosity, Bob decides to check how his mutual fund investment is doing.

So, instead of looking at his portfolio, he opens a finance website that reports that his fund has not been doing that well. In fact, it seems to have made only about 2% of profit in the last 1 year.

Worried about his money, Bob then opens up his actual account and checks. To his horror, he did not even make 2% that the MF made. For some reason his invested amount seems to have gone down too.

But, Bob convinces himself that it's all just a temporary decline and so he continues to put in some money into the MF each month. He decides to give it some more time and so he does not check his mutual fund portfolio for another 2 years.

Now, he again opens up the finance website, and to his delight, the fund has made a little over 10% in the last 3 years.

Excitingly, Bob opens up his account. But, strangely, he seems to have made much less. In fact, by his calculations, he only made about 6%.

And then Bob decides to pull out the money from this mutual fund. He sells the fund. Luckily, there was no exit load on the money he invested for the first two years, but there is an exit load on the money he invested in the last one year.

And so after getting his money back, he realizes that he really got a return of just 3% on his money.

But, wait there is some more bad news. He owes some money to the IRS now. And then

Bob completely goes berserk within his mind. "You know, I could have made that much money if I had simply put it in a savings account" Well Bob, what can I tell you? That's just what happens to a lot of MF "buyers" every day.

Of course, there are other ways to invest money in MFs. But, the only real commitment you need is to ensure that you don't "trade" in MFs, rather you invest. Make yourself rich, not your broker.

Don't pay fees where you don't really have to. And be on the guard, because ultimately, the only person who wants you to not pay fees is YOU. Everyone else would prefer to part you from your money. Don't let them do that.

Of course, I pay a crazy amount of fees to a certain fund. I will not go into much detail. But, the fact is that he makes me 40% richer every year, so if he takes a cut I don't mind.

But, the small investor doesn't really make 40%. Small investors do not qualify for that fund. But, even after earning 40%, I don't just divest my money out of the fund. No.

That would cost me some serious money in taxes and fees. Both of which I don't want to do. So, high fees is justified if you get a high return. But since most MF managers don't even perform as well as the overall index, all investors would be much better investing in index funds.

But WAIT! Usually, some readers would have by now opened up various websites, looking for an index fund. Hold on. Not every index fund is "good". "Aaah! There is a catch!"

Of course there is. With all these people drumming it into our years, "invest in index funds, invest in index funds." There must be something in it for them. So let me give you the detail that you deserve.

I think the following small piece of information is worth more than this book actually cost. So listen up:

Index Funds generally claim to track stock market indexes. For example, Vanguard S&P 500 tracks the S&P 500. But, there is a catch.

The fact is, not all funds track the underlying securities in an index correctly. Without complicating matters for you, let us just understand it this way.

Say there are 50 stocks in a certain index, and an index funds decides to track these 50 securities. Well, how should the 50 stocks be bought? What should be the volume of the stocks bought? When should one exit and enter a stock?

Because, at times, some stocks are removed from certain indexes, and are replaced by other stocks.

Due to all these complications, it may be that while the index makes a steady 10%, your index fund only makes 6%! Of course, I may be exaggerating, but you need to ensure that the gap is as minimum as possible between how the index is performing and how the index fund that you are interested in, is performing.

Contrary to popular belief, for index funds, past performance is indicative of future returns. Without making any specific claims about specific fund, I would request you to research for yourself. It's not rocket science.

If you are more of a visual person, then open up the charts of the index and the index fund, placing them vertically on the screen.

You can then compare to see if the fund has efficiently tracked the actual index over the past many years. If you understand numbers better, then track the growth of the index and compare it to the return provided by the index fund.

Generally, if a fund has been able to successfully track an index for five years or more, you would be able to make money investing in it. This is a simple process and it's not rocket science. Anybody can do that. Once you find such an index fund, invest in that one fund consistently.

So, build wealth by staying invested so that you don't have to pay short term taxes, or fees. Find a cheaper broker if you can. I'll not repeat the information that is already out there.

But, let us say that your ultimate goal is to build up a corpus of a million dollars. You start investing $400 monthly at 10% .a. but you also pay 1% fees annually too.

You reach your goal in about 30 years. If you had saved that 1%, then you would have made the same amount of money in 26.5 years. 3.5 years is a lot of time.

And then if you don't trade often, you don't have to pay extra taxes, and such. And all those factors combined actually helps you achieve your goals within 20 years! Now that is something isn't it?

You should always remember, the financial institutions never really want you to know this fact, but it extremely important to remember, that no matter what financial situation you are in, as long as you have a good cash flow, you'd be able to pay down your debts in 3 to 5 years. For extraneous cases, the period may be up to 7 years.

But, the point is, if you could pay down your debt while you are investing, which is what most companies do as well, you would be able to increase your monthly contributions towards your goals as well.

I don't have to tell you what would happen if you were able to increase your $400 contribution by even a couple of hundred dollars.

The fact is that even your craziest financial goals are achievable within 10-20 years, if you put your heart and soul into it. Of course, I don't recommend starving yourself so as to become a millionaire sooner, but I can tell you that I never did mind going hungry during my days of struggle.

The point is, you should invest in equity for at least 10 years and every time you get a raise or every time you are able to pay off some debt, direct the money you used for EMIs towards your portfolio. Sky isn't even the limit. There is no limit.

Financial abundance requires some short term sacrifices, and if that is required, do it, but achieve your goal.

Greed is not Good

Look, we all get cocky when we make a hefty profit. As if we had anything to do with the way a certain stock performed. And we all get a little scared when we see our net worth going down significantly. It's human nature.

But, greed and fear must not drive your investment decisions. If you have chickened out of a stock in the past, only to see it rise suddenly soon after. Or if you have bought a stock at its highest point, only to see it go down the dumps. You should know by now, why greed is not good and fear is not helpful.

That's why, if you don't have the ability to control your emotions, do not directly invest in the stock market. You would be saving yourself a ton of money. Plus, you would not have to lie to yourself about why something did not work out.

Personally, I think people should invest in closed ended funds. But, unfortunately, the managers of closed ended funds do not really do as well as those managing open ended funds.

I guess it's all about motivation – a closed ended fund manager knows that investors can't pull their money out when they wish, so he takes a chill pill while investors get a heart attack.

But, still, I recommend that you invest in ways that would significantly reduce your chances of getting out of an investment by just clicking a button on some fancy website.

This is important because staying investing is the ultimate principle of investing. Buy today sell never is a good principle too. You just have to remember that a few stocks of funds will go down and a few stocks will go up. But, neither of these events means anything to an investor.

Think of it like this: If you went out today and bought a fancy meteor for a $100 bucks and placed that rock in your living room, do you really care what that rock is worth the next day?

All you wanted to do was keep something from outer space in your living room, and you now have that thing in your living room. You want nothing else.

So, would you fret about whether the rock is worth more or less? No you won't. Take the example from Peter Lynch's famous book, if you had bought a house, would you call up your broker every half an hour to check the price of the house? Would you sell or buy the house based on that data.

Of course you won't. The same rule applies towards any investment. You don't just get out because of fear or greed. A lot of people suffered due to the sub-prime crisis. A lot of people lost their homes.

But, think about the people who did not lose their homes. Do you think their lives changed because of the price of their houses going up or down? They had a roof on their heads and were able to afford the mortgages, they did not care what the price of the house next door was!

Similarly, ultimately if you have bought a stock at $100, it doesn't matter whether it goes down to $10 or if it goes up to $200. None of that matters, unless you sell!

If you sell at $10 you take a loss, and if you sell at $200 you make a profit. If you have diversified, you won't face significant issues.

MY EXPERIMENTS WITH BONDS

Warren Buffet once called derivatives, "Weapons of mass destruction". Why? Because derivatives that inherently use some form of leverage, not only pose a threat to the investors, but also to the economy at large.

Just like complex derivatives can be termed as WMDs, Bonds can be called the "Weapons of Mass Prosperity". If we did not have the ability to borrow money, very few of us would have been able to afford the luxuries that we take for granted today.

People would have lost their motivation. Think about it – if you thought that you would be able to buy your first car only after 7 years of saving money, you might not work as hard.

But, debt allows you to go out there and buy your favorite toy for just 10% down or 20% down. Consumer credit allows you to buy that latest crazy gadget that you love so much. You buy a house using debt too. So, debt is everywhere and it is good.

Just like people borrow money, companies and governments borrow money as well. In order to borrow money from people, they issue bonds at a certain interest rate. This interest rate is known as coupon rate.

Just like in any debt transaction, there are two parties involved: The Lender and The Borrower. Clearly, at the end of the debt repayment process, the lender will be richer in terms of money, but the borrower would also have been able to create value by using the money that it had borrowed.

Bonds are safer as compared to stocks and mutual funds because they have a fixed interest rate attached to them. Governments generally do not default on their payments.

And if a company defaults on its payments, the borrowers get to liquidate the company's assets and get their money back that way.

So, either way, the lenders generally do get their money back. The only exception to this rule are the airline companies across the world, who sometimes take on so much debt, and yet are not able to pay those debts back. Even after liquidation, investors don't always get their money back.

Now, as explained a bond has an interest rate component attached to it. This is known as a coupon rate. Bonds, just like stocks can be traded on the open market. As a result the price of bonds also varies. This can be beneficial or not so beneficial for the investor.

In order to explain this concept in a simple manner, let us use an example:

Suppose Company 'C' decides to raise money by issuing bonds. It says that it will issue 100 bonds for the price of $100 per bond. The company promises to pay 10% per annum on the bond, i.e. $10 per annum.

At the end of 3 years, the company will return the $100 that it had taken initially. That sounds like a simple loan that consumers generally take from a bank.

Now a hundred investors buy 1-1 bond each, and then the bond starts trading in the open market. Suppose, the price of the bond itself comes down to $90 per bond.

Mr. Slick purchases bonds of Company 'C' at $90. But, Slick has outdone himself. The company is still paying $10 a year. So instead of getting 10%, Slick is now able to get 11%. But, that's not all.

At the end of three years, Company 'C' buys back its bonds at $100, hence repaying its 'loan'. So, not only does Slick make $30 per bond as interest, he also gets an additional $10 per bond at the closure of the 'loan'.

Well I don't know how simpler I could have made that example. I had to hold back a lot of information, just so that all readers could understand the example.

Now, the terms involved with bonds are:

Coupon rate: In the above example, 10%

Yield to Maturity: In the above example, 11%

Face value: $100

Those are the 3 basic terms that you should know. Every time you analyze a bond, always look at the YTM (yield to maturity) because that is what you'll be getting back from your investment as interest.

Also, some bonds do not promise return of the initial investment. Some bonds pay interests annually, while others pay interest on a monthly basis. Some even pay weekly.

There are a lot of different things to check before you invest in a bond. Read the related documents yourself to know complete details for the bond. This is extremely important.

Also, the above example is over simplified. Bonds generally require you to buy at least

10 bonds at (say) $1000 each. And so you need a good amount of cash to invest in bonds and stay invested.

The only way to lose money by investing in bonds, is if your bond is paying you less than what inflation is taking away. Otherwise, Bonds are the best form of investment out there, if you don't want to lose a penny and make a buck while you're at it.

There are also NCDs, CCDs, Treasury bonds, Municipal bonds, Junk Bonds, etc. etc. You need to understand these yourself, because even if I tell you, you won't know what I am talking about. Self-study is encouraged when it comes to bonds.

If you don't understand the fuss about bonds, here is a simple fact. If you invested $100 in a bond at 10%, you will double your investment in 7 years and then again double that in just 5. Compounding works at a larger scale if you have time on your side.

Here is another fact to remember: Always opt for compounding twice a year or more, if you are given an option. Compounding once a year is good, so twice must be better, right? Right. Compounding twice a year will only help you achieve your goals faster.